GRETA
THUNBERG

AND THE
CLIMATE
CRISIS

AMY
CHAPMAN

W
FRANKLIN
WATTS

Franklin Watts
First published in Great Britain in 2020 by The Watts Publishing Group
Copyright © The Watts Publishing Group, 2020

Produced for Franklin Watts by
White-Thomson Publishing Ltd
www.wtpub.co.uk

HB ISBN: 978 1 4451 7289 7
PB ISBN: 978 1 4451 7290 3

Credits
Editor: Izzi Howell
Designer: Dan Prescott, Couper Street Type Co.

The publisher would like to thank the following for permission to reproduce their pictures:
Alamy: Jasper Chamber cover, Mark Kerrison/Alamy Live News 21, CTK Photo/Grzegorz Klatka 23,
Lora Grigorova/Alamy Live News 38t; Getty: MALIN HOELSTAD/SVD/TT/TT NEWS AGENCY/AFP
4, Vladimir Zapletin 7t, JONATHAN NACKSTRAND/AFP 9, dovate 14, Iborisoff 18t, NOAH SEELAM/
AFP 24t, JOHANNES EISELE/AFP 27, Ron Adar/SOPA Images/LightRocket 28, Spencer Platt 29,
KIRSTY O'CONNOR/POOL/AFP 32, Horacio Villalobos 33, LUIS TATO/AFP 42; Shutterstock:
Meilun 5t, Nightman1965 5b, Daniele COSSU 6, mart 7b, Per Grunditz 8t, 20 and 37b, mghstars and
Gaidamashchuk 8b, nicostock 10, infinetsoft 11, Gary Whitton 12, trgrowth 13, 3xy 15, Zephyr_p
16t, Claudia Pylinskaya 16b, xuanhuongho 17, Sabangvideo 18b, DES82 19t, Andrew Chin 19b, Holli
22, MicroOne 24b, Liv Oeian 25, lev radin 30, MSPhotographic 31t, mountain beetle 31b, ph_m and
Photography Stock Ruiz 34, Alexandros Michailidis 35, Liv Oeian 36, Sattalat phukkum 37t, vladwel
38b, Free Wind 2014 39, majeczka 40, Robert Paul Laschon, Vitaly Art, SkyPics Studio, Tako design
and all_is_magic 41, Denis Burdin 43, Rawpixel.com 44, photocosmos1 45.

All design elements from Shutterstock.

Every attempt has been made to clear copyright. Should there be any
inadvertent omission please apply to the publisher for rectification.

Printed in Dubai

Franklin Watts
An imprint of
Hachette Children's Group
Part of The Watts Publishing Group
Carmelite House
50 Victoria Embankment
London EC4Y 0DZ

An Hachette UK Company
www.hachette.co.uk
www.franklinwatts.co.uk

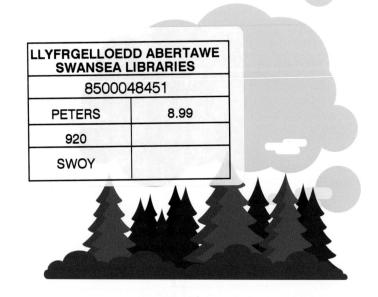

CONTENTS

MEET GRETA THUNBERG

Every day, we are surrounded by news of the climate crisis that our planet is facing. It's very easy to feel overwhelmed or powerless. What can just one person do to help save our planet? Greta Thunberg is proof that anyone can make a difference, after her incredible journey from lone climate protester to spearhead of an international environmental movement.

Early life

Greta was born on 3 January 2003 in Stockholm, Sweden. Her mother, Malena, is a famous opera singer in Sweden, while her father, Svante, is an actor. She also has a younger sister named Beata. When Greta was young, Malena often went on tour, performing concerts across Europe. The whole family, including Greta, would join her, flying from country to country.

→
*Greta with her
mother, Malena*

Finding out

At the age of eight, Greta learned about climate change for the first time. She was shocked and scared. She felt frustrated by suggestions of small things that everyone could do to help 'solve' the climate crisis, such as turning off lights or reusing paper, as these didn't seem like they'd have much impact. Greta couldn't understand why there was such little action about climate change on a large, global scale, such as making it illegal to burn fossil fuels.

JUST 20 FOSSIL FUEL COMPANIES ARE DIRECTLY LINKED TO 35 PER CENT OF ALL ENERGY-RELATED GREENHOUSE GAS EMISSIONS.

→

It is not just the burning of fossil fuels for energy that produces greenhouse gases and pollution; the energy used to extract and transport them also damages the environment.

A diagnosis

At the age of 11, Greta became depressed and stopped eating and talking. She was diagnosed with Asperger's, OCD and selective mutism, which means that she only speaks when necessary. Today, Greta sees her diagnosis of Asperger's as a superpower (see page 36) because it means that she often sees things in 'black or white', allowing her to clearly see the importance of our planet's health above other issues. This is one of the reasons why she is so passionately convinced that solving the climate crisis is the most important issue facing our society at the moment.

→

Greta's selective mutism does not affect her ability to speak expressively and clearly in public. She finds it easier to talk about subjects that she considers important.

'EVERYONE KEEPS SAYING THAT CLIMATE CHANGE IS ... THE MOST IMPORTANT ISSUE OF ALL, AND YET THEY JUST CARRY ON LIKE BEFORE. I DON'T UNDERSTAND THAT BECAUSE IF THE EMISSIONS HAVE TO STOP, THEN WE MUST STOP THE EMISSIONS.'

GRETA THUNBERG, 2018

Family changes

Greta's passion for fighting against climate change has had a big impact on her family life. Before she started her global campaigning, she inspired her entire family to change their lifestyle and become more environmentally conscious. Previously, the whole family often travelled by plane to accompany Greta's mother on tour. But once Greta learned of the environmental impact of flights, she persuaded her family to stop flying. This meant that her mother had to give up her international opera career. Greta also convinced her family to follow a vegan diet for environmental reasons.

→
Large-scale cattle farms, such as this one, contribute to global warming because the cows release methane in their burps and farts, which is a greenhouse gas (see page 13).

58 PER CENT OF GREENHOUSE GAS EMISSIONS CREATED BY FOOD PRODUCTION COME FROM ANIMAL PRODUCTS, SO VEGANISM CAN BE A SIMPLE WAY OF MAKING YOUR DIET MORE ENVIRONMENTALLY FRIENDLY.

GOING ON STRIKE

By late August 2018, Greta had had enough of hearing about the climate crisis. Sweden was experiencing its hottest summer since records began, along with heatwaves and wildfires. She decided that she had to do something to draw attention to the climate crisis and politicians' unwillingness to address it. So Greta decided to go on strike.

Planning to strike

The idea for Greta's strike was simple. She wouldn't go to school until the Swedish elections, which were taking place on 9 September 2018. Her strike was inspired by students in the USA, who had stopped going to school to protest against school shootings and the lack of action taken to prevent further attacks. Greta didn't want her strike to go unnoticed, so she sat outside the parliament buildings in Stockholm, the capital of Sweden, during school hours.

SKOLSTREJK FÖR KLIMATET

IN JULY 2018, TEMPERATURES ACROSS SCANDINAVIA WERE 10°C ABOVE AVERAGE.

↑
Greta carried a large sign saying 'School strike for the climate' in Swedish and handed out leaflets explaining her strike to passers-by.

Joining in

Right from the start, people were inspired by Greta's strike. A few of them joined Greta outside parliament to protest. However, not everyone agreed with her strike. A few people made comments in the street when they passed her. Her parents and some of her teachers were worried about her missing school, but Greta did lots of homework and read books while on strike.

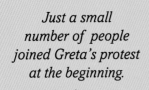

Just a small number of people joined Greta's protest at the beginning.

↓

'... WE RESPECT THAT SHE WANTS TO MAKE A STAND. SHE CAN EITHER SIT AT HOME AND BE REALLY UNHAPPY, OR PROTEST AND BE HAPPY.'

SVANTE THUNBERG, 2018

FridaysforFuture

On 7 September 2018, just before the Swedish elections, Greta decided to make a change to her school strike. Instead of striking every day, she would now be striking every Friday. Greta called her new strike FridaysforFuture. This slogan would go on to be used on posters, hashtags and signs around the world, uniting many people with the same message.

A FridaysforFuture sign at a student protest in Italy.

The Paris Agreement

One of the main aims of Greta's strike was to pressure Sweden to change its behaviour until it was in line with the Paris Agreement. This is an international treaty signed in 2016 that aims to limit the increase in global temperature to 1.5°C this century. Countries that sign the treaty are required to limit greenhouse gas emissions and preserve areas that reduce greenhouse gases, such as forests (see page 12). Developed countries must help developing countries to achieve these goals.

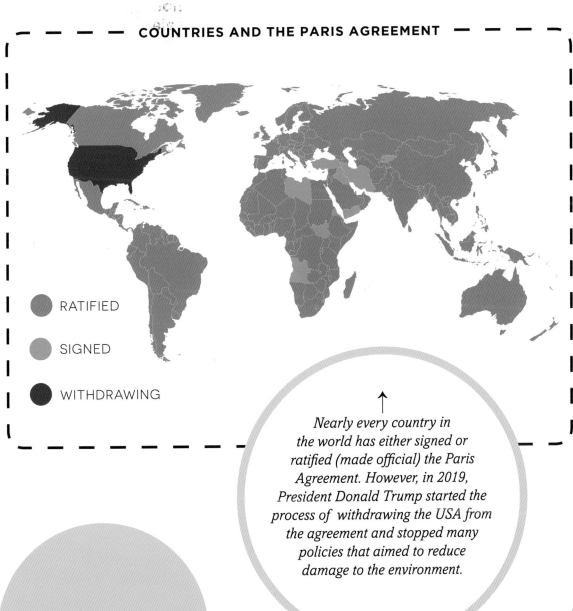

COUNTRIES AND THE PARIS AGREEMENT

RATIFIED

SIGNED

WITHDRAWING

Nearly every country in the world has either signed or ratified (made official) the Paris Agreement. However, in 2019, President Donald Trump started the process of withdrawing the USA from the agreement and stopped many policies that aimed to reduce damage to the environment.

THE CLIMATE CRISIS

Greta's goal is to raise awareness of the climate emergency affecting our planet. She wants everyone to put pressure on governments and big businesses to make meaningful changes to reduce our impact on the planet. But how have we got ourselves into this crisis and what is the scale of these environmental problems?

Human activity

Many different human activities are contributing to the climate crisis, including burning fossil fuels, vehicle exhausts and large-scale farming. These activities all release greenhouse gases (see page 13) and air pollution. Deforestation is also a major issue. Cutting down trees destroys the habitats of wild animals and plants and means that there are fewer trees to absorb extra carbon dioxide from the atmosphere.

$\rightarrow$

A coal-fired power plant in Utah, USA. The USA is one of the top carbon dioxide emitters in the world.

The greenhouse effect

The increase in temperature on Earth (global warming) is due to the greenhouse effect. Greenhouse gases, including carbon dioxide, methane and water vapour, gather in the atmosphere around Earth and block some heat from the Sun from escaping into space. This increases the surface temperature on Earth.

The greenhouse effect is a natural process. Without it, Earth would be too cold for life. Natural greenhouse gases are released by animals breathing, volcanoes, wetlands, the water cycle and other sources. However, the greenhouses gases released by human activity are making the layer of gases thicker, increasing the amount of heat being trapped by the greenhouse effect and making the temperature rise far beyond healthy levels.

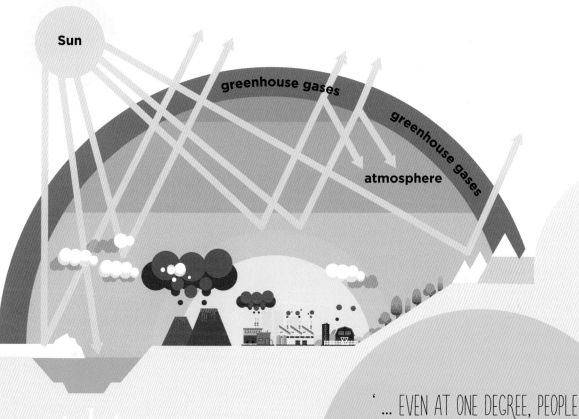

Sun

greenhouse gases

greenhouse gases

atmosphere

THE AVERAGE SURFACE TEMPERATURE ON EARTH HAS RISEN 0.9°C SINCE THE LATE NINETEENTH CENTURY.

' ... EVEN AT ONE DEGREE, PEOPLE ARE DYING FROM THE CLIMATE CRISIS ... OUR GREENHOUSE GAS EMISSIONS [HAVE] TO STOP. TO STAY BELOW 1.5 DEGREES.'

GRETA THUNBERG, 2019

Hot and cold

Global warming is affecting our climate in many ways. It is causing more extreme weather – not just hotter but also unusually cold weather in some areas. This is because warmer temperatures at the poles are affecting the movement of cold air and sending it further away than normal.

2016 WAS THE WARMEST YEAR ON RECORD, FOLLOWED BY 2019. THE DECADE FROM 2010–2019 WAS THE HOTTEST EVER RECORDED.

→

Many northern cities experienced extreme cold weather in the winter of 2019, partly as a result of global warming.

Extreme weather

Higher temperatures on Earth affect the water cycle. When it's hot, more water evaporates from the ground, meaning that more water falls as rain later. This leads to heavy rain but also drought, as less water remains in the soil. Tropical storms and hurricanes are also more likely to occur.

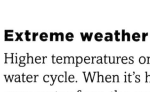

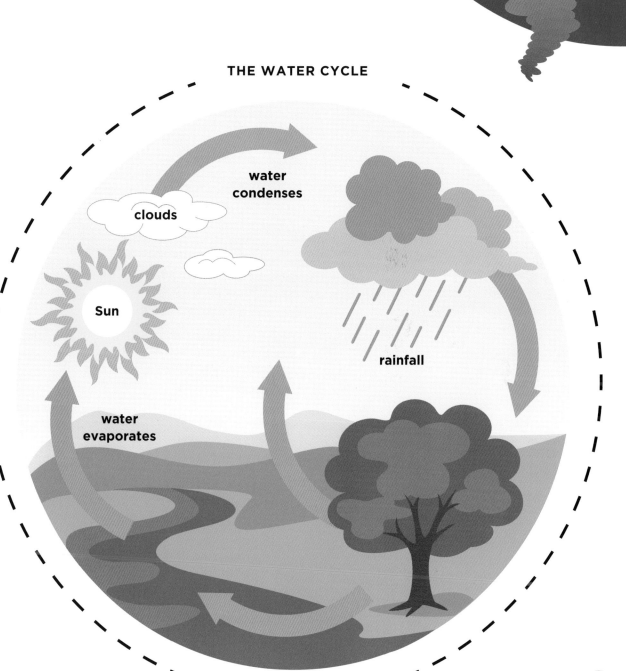

THE WATER CYCLE

clouds

water condenses

Sun

rainfall

water evaporates

Polar problems

Global warming is particularly affecting the polar regions. Ice at the poles is melting quickly into the ocean. This is having a devastating impact on polar wildlife that rest and hunt on the sea ice, such as polar bears. With nowhere to live or catch food, these animals are being forced out of their natural polar habitat and dying.

Ice is melting on land and at sea in polar regions.

↓

ARCTIC SEA ICE HAS DECREASED BY 10 PER CENT IN THE PAST 30 YEARS.

Flood warning

Melting polar ice is making sea levels rise around the world. As a result, low-lying coastal areas are flooding more often. Many of these places are in less economically developed countries in South and Southeast Asia, such as Bangladesh, Thailand and Vietnam. However, if global warming continues, many more low areas around the world will also be affected.

Flooding in Ho Chi Minh City, Vietnam

↓

Oceans and oxygen

Global warming is affecting oxygen levels in the oceans, as warm water holds less oxygen than cool water. This threatens ocean animals, such as fish, that take oxygen from sea water through their gills. Species that are more tolerant to low oxygen levels, such as jellyfish, are dominating and disrupting ocean ecosystems as a result.

Acidic oceans

Greenhouse gases, such as carbon dioxide, are also making the ocean more acidic. The ocean has always absorbed carbon dioxide, currently taking in around 40 per cent of what we emit. The more carbon dioxide we release, the more the oceans absorb and the more acidic the water becomes. Acidic water damages coral reefs and the shells of ocean animals, such as oysters.

Healthy coral reef

Bleached coral reef

↑
← *Higher ocean temperatures are causing coral reef bleaching. When water is too warm, algae that lives within the coral becomes stressed and leaves. This makes coral appear white. As algae are the main food source for the coral, bleached coral goes hungry and is more vulnerable to disease.*

A biodiverse world?

Wildlife in every ecosystem is greatly affected by the climate crisis. Global warming is destroying their habitats and food sources, leading to starvation and death. Animal and plant populations are falling and some scientists believe we are facing a mass extinction, where many different species will die out. If this continues, we will lose the biodiversity that makes our planet so unique.

↑

Many animal species, such as bees, are key to human survival as they pollinate crops, such as apples. If these species become extinct, our food supply will be seriously threatened.

'HARDLY ANYONE SPEAK[S] ABOUT THE FACT THAT WE ARE IN THE MIDST OF THE SIXTH MASS EXTINCTION ... THAT THE EXTINCTION RATE IS TODAY BETWEEN 1,000 AND 10,000 TIMES HIGHER THAN WHAT IS SEEN AS NORMAL.'

GRETA THUNBERG, 2019

ANIMALS, SUCH AS INSECTS, BIRDS AND BATS ARE RESPONSIBLE FOR POLLINATING 35 PER CENT OF ALL FOOD CROPS.

INSPIRING OTHERS

As Greta's message was so urgent, impacting everyone on the planet, news of her strike quickly spread on social media and in traditional forms of media, such as newspapers, radio and TV news programmes. Greta's actions inspired many other people, especially young people, to take part in similar events. Her protest grew from a small, individual strike in Sweden to a global movement.

Shared around the world

When Greta started her protest in August 2018, she posted about it on Instagram and Twitter. Her posts were shared by other social media accounts, and then quickly picked up by local and international news reporters. In just over a week, Greta's story had made it around the world.

Many news channels sent reporters to Sweden to interview Greta and report on her protest.

↓

A wider audience

This media coverage gave Greta new opportunities to spread the message of the environmental dangers that we face. By October 2018, she was speaking in front of 10,000 people at a climate change march in Finland organised by two major environmental charities – Greenpeace and the World Wildlife Foundation. In November, she gave a TED talk in Stockholm that was shared across the world on the TED Youtube channel, which has millions of subscribers.

↑

On 31 October 2018, Greta attended and spoke at a climate protest in London, UK. She was already an environmental celebrity, only two months after she started her strike.

Finding followers

Young people around the world were inspired by Greta's message and decided to join her school strikes. By December 2018, just months after Greta first decided to go on strike, 20,000 students had taken part in similar climate protests. These protests took place in at least 270 towns and cities in Belgium, the UK, the USA, Japan, Australia, Canada and many other countries.

'YOU DONT HAVE TO SCHOOL STRIKE, IT'S YOUR OWN CHOICE. BUT WHY SHOULD WE BE STUDYING FOR A FUTURE THAT SOON MAY BE NO MORE? THIS IS MORE IMPORTANT THAN SCHOOL, I THINK.'

GRETA THUNBERG, 2018

→ Students on a school strike rally in Sydney, Australia, in November 2018. Thousands of students took part, despite the Australian prime minister Scott Morrison urging them to be 'less activist'.

The United Nations

Greta's message and fame quickly spread and opened up opportunities for her. One of her earliest international appearances was at the 2018 United Nations Climate Change Conference in Poland. In her speech, she criticised the negotiators at the conference who were trying to agree on rules as part of the Paris Agreement. Greta believed that they weren't doing enough to make significant changes and that they were leaving a terrible burden for the next generation.

↑

Greta took part in a press conference during the United Nations climate conference in December 2018. News agencies around the world were very keen to interview her.

Students on strike in Hyderabad, India, on 15 March 2019. →

The Global Climate Strikes

On 15 March 2019, many children around the world left school to protest for their future at the first Global Climate Strike. They demanded that politicians listen and take action against climate change. Many of the protests took place in less economically developed countries, such as the Philippines, which are most affected by the impact of climate change (see pages 14–19).

The second Global Climate Strike took place on 24 May 2019. Greta attended the strikes in Europe, keeping her promise not to fly and only travel by public transport or other green alternatives.

'WE ARE JUST PASSING ON THE WORDS OF THE SCIENCE. OUR ONLY DEMAND IS THAT YOU START LISTENING TO IT, AND THEN START ACTING.'

GRETA THUNBERG, 2019

NO MORE FOSSIL FUELS

MORE THAN 1.4 MILLION PEOPLE TOOK PART IN THE FIRST GLOBAL CLIMATE STRIKE IN OVER 2,200 TOWNS AND CITIES IN OVER 120 COUNTRIES.

SAVE THE PLANET

A voice for the youth

The success of the Global Climate Strikes put Greta even further into the spotlight. She became a regular guest at hugely influential climate meetings and shared the stage with many important leaders at events such as the World Economic Forum and at the European Parliament.

Greta was invited to these events because world leaders wanted to hear her input. It is very unusual for politicians to give this kind of platform to a 16-year-old. But it is clear that Greta has an important perspective that represents the thoughts of her generation and therefore must be listened to.

'THE FACT THAT SHE WAS 16, AND I WAS 16 AS WELL, AND SHE COULD DO SUCH AMAZING THINGS AND CHANGE THE WORLD, IT MADE ME THINK WE CAN ALL DO IT AS WELL.'

XIYE BASTIDA, YOUTH CLIMATE ACTIVIST, 2019

Greta joins school strikers in Stockholm, Sweden, in April 2019.
↓

ACROSS THE ATLANTIC

On 28 August 2019, Greta Thunberg arrived in New York Harbour after 15 days at sea on an 18-metre racing yacht. After leaving Plymouth, UK, on 14 August, she had experienced rough Atlantic storms and gone over a fortnight with no toilet or shower access. But why make this difficult and uncomfortable journey when these two countries are just eight hours apart by plane?

Travel dilemmas

When Greta was invited to speak at the UN summit on zero emissions in New York, USA, she had a transport problem on her hands. Previously, she had travelled around Europe by train, which is a method of transport that releases a fairly small amount of carbon. However, the long journey from Europe to North America is typically made by plane. She knew that she couldn't justify the carbon emissions from her flight, so she had to find an alternative.

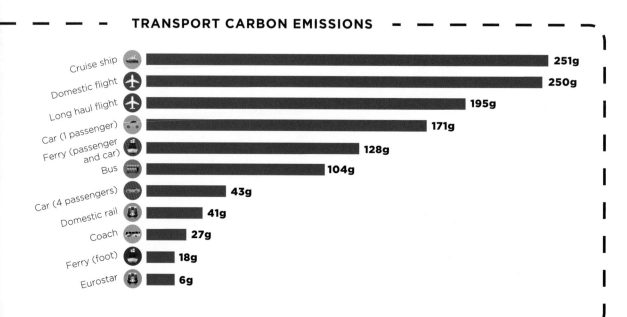

TRANSPORT CARBON EMISSIONS

Transport	Emissions
Cruise ship	251g
Domestic flight	250g
Long haul flight	195g
Car (1 passenger)	171g
Ferry (passenger and car)	128g
Bus	104g
Car (4 passengers)	43g
Domestic rail	41g
Coach	27g
Ferry (foot)	18g
Eurostar	6g

Greta completed the Atlantic crossing with her father, a cameraman and two members of crew.

↓

Green globe-trotting

The solution came in the form of the *Malizia II* yacht, which was offered to Greta by its captain and team. The *Malizia II* is a zero-carbon boat that is propelled by wind. Solar panels and hydro-generators produce electricity for lights and communication systems on board. The boat was built for around-the-world races, so the trip across the Atlantic wouldn't be an issue for its crew.

A RETURN FLIGHT FROM LONDON TO NEW YORK RELEASES 0.67 TONNES OF CARBON DIOXIDE PER PASSENGER. THAT'S 11 PER CENT OF WHAT AN AVERAGE PERSON IN THE UK EMITS IN ONE YEAR.

Protests in the streets

Days before the UN climate summit, around 4 million people around the world took to the streets to protest against the climate crisis. Greta joined the 250,000 protesters in New York. She made a speech in which she explained that the climate strikes were just the beginning of global change. A climate revolution was coming, whether people liked it or not!

Many supporters came to watch Greta's speech in New York.

↓

Powerful words

On 23 September 2019, Greta attended the United Nations climate summit. She joined world leaders and representatives from many countries. Greta made a passionate speech that immediately went viral around the world. Many people connected with her frustration and rage that politicians and global businesses weren't taking the climate crisis seriously, and therefore were putting young people's future at risk.

'WE ARE IN THE BEGINNING OF A MASS EXTINCTION, AND ALL YOU CAN TALK ABOUT IS MONEY AND FAIRY TALES OF ETERNAL ECONOMIC GROWTH. HOW DARE YOU!'

GRETA THUNBERG, 2019

Can't change, won't change

Before the summit, Greta predicted that many world leaders would not be prepared to make the extreme changes needed to pull us back from climate disaster. Sadly, she was correct. The spokesperson from China, one of the world's largest polluters, did not put forward any plans to help tackle climate change. Representatives from other major polluters, such as the USA and Brazil, did not even speak at the summit.

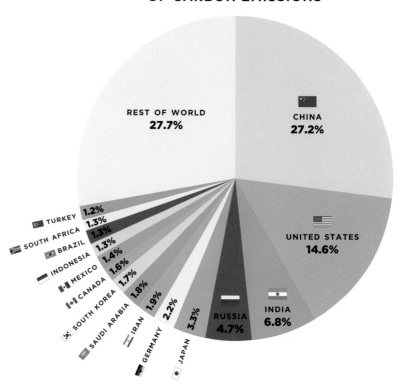

TOP 15 GREATEST POLLUTERS OF CARBON EMISSIONS

REST OF WORLD
27.7%

CHINA
27.2%

UNITED STATES
14.6%

INDIA
6.8%

RUSSIA
4.7%

JAPAN 3.3%

GERMANY 2.2%

IRAN 1.9%

SAUDI ARABIA 1.8%

SOUTH KOREA 1.7%

CANADA 1.6%

MEXICO 1.4%

INDONESIA 1.3%

BRAZIL 1.3%

SOUTH AFRICA 1.3%

TURKEY 1.2%

An American absence

US President Donald Trump briefly attended the summit, but left early. Some people think Trump's absence shows how little he cares about climate change and the planet's wellbeing. Trump has often shown a lack of understanding about climate change, and he has questioned climate science that is widely accepted by scientists on several occasions.

→
Trump left the climate summit to attend another meeting that he had organised.

Tweets and trolling

On the night of 23 September, Trump tweeted about Greta, describing her as 'a very happy young girl looking forward to a bright and wonderful future'. This could be seen as mocking Greta's serious concerns about the future, as well as dismissing her as just a young girl. However, Greta made a joke out of Trump's trolling by changing her Twitter biography to Trump's description of her. She prefers to respond calmly and maturely to those who criticise her work (see page 37).

LIAR LIAR
THE PLANET'S ON FIRE

$\rightarrow$
Many protestors at the climate strike were angry about Trump's attitude towards the climate crisis.

AT LEAST 97 PER CENT OF CLIMATE SCIENTISTS AGREE THAT RECENT CLIMATE CHANGE IS DUE TO HUMAN ACTIVITY.

NEXT STEPS

Greta Thunberg continues to go from strength to strength. She has already opened the eyes of many people around the world, particularly young people, to the reality of climate change. Her future is filled with exciting opportunities to spread her message and continue to make a difference.

The power of voting

Greta is very vocal about the importance of voting if you care about the climate crisis. Choosing politicians who will take climate change seriously and act accordingly is crucial, as they are some of the only people who have the power to make significant changes. Unfortunately, in most countries, young people aren't able to vote and choose their leaders until the age of 18. Many think that the voting age should be lowered to 16.

In the run-up to the 2019 general elections in the UK, leaders from the Conservative party and the Brexit party failed to attend a debate about climate change. They were replaced with melting ice statues as a symbol of the parties' presumed lack of interest in discussing this important topic.

↓

As well as attending the UN climate summit in the USA, Greta had planned to attend the COP25 United Nations Climate Change Conference in Santiago, Chile, to make her trip across the Atlantic worthwhile. However, when the conference was moved to Spain, Greta had another dilemma on her hands. It had been tricky to find one ride across the Atlantic, let alone two!

Luckily, her social media following came to the rescue and she managed to get a ride back to Europe with a family who were sailing around the world on their boat. They left the USA on 13 November and arrived in Lisbon, Portugal, three weeks later.

→ Members of the press came out to meet Greta and the rest of the ship's crew when they landed in Portugal.

Not listening

At the COP25 climate conference, Greta expressed concern that the massive climate protest movement has achieved nothing, as greenhouse gas emissions have continued to rise. She said that young people would continue to strike until action is taken – although they would rather not have to! Young people from developing nations also attended the conference to share their personal experiences of how climate change is affecting their country, for example higher levels of disease due to wetter, warmer weather.

'WE CAN'T GO ON LIKE THIS; IT IS NOT SUSTAINABLE THAT CHILDREN SKIP SCHOOL AND WE DON'T WANT TO CONTINUE ... PEOPLE ARE SUFFERING AND DYING TODAY. WE CAN'T WAIT ANY LONGER.'

GRETA THUNBERG, 2019

Around 500,000 people attended protests in Madrid to raise awareness of the climate crisis.

↓

A big year

In December 2019, Greta was named *Time* magazine's person of the year. She is the youngest person ever to receive this honour.

Greta's phrase 'climate strike' was also named the word of the year by Collin's Dictionary, after the dictionary observed that it was used hundreds of times more than in previous years.

→
In 2019, Greta took part in countless protests and marches and gave many inspirational speeches.

DIFFERENT AND PROUD

Greta believes that her Asperger's syndrome is partly to thank for her incredible passion when addressing the climate crisis. To her, it is a superpower! However, she regularly faces criticism from some important people for her beliefs, her personality and her lifestyle.

An unexpected gift

In the past, Greta struggled with her diagnosis of Asperger's (a condition that can make communication and social interaction more challenging). She didn't tell other people that she had Asperger's because she knew that some people saw it as something negative.

However, Greta's interest in climate change helped her to see her Asperger's as a gift, as it gave her the focus and motivation to make a significant impact on a global scale. She sees things in clear, but urgent, terms. For example, Greta sees that the climate crisis has to be solved, or our society as we know it will end.

Greta's dedication to raising awareness of environmental issues, partly thanks to her Asperger's, gave her the courage and conviction to begin her protest alone.

↓

Cruel words

Sadly, a few people have used Greta's diagnosis as a reason to criticise her. Greta often turns around these comments and makes fun of them on Twitter. She believes that these people make personal attacks because they don't have any scientific arguments or real reasons to criticise her!

Anyone can post almost anything on Twitter, which can make it a source of cyberbullying and personal attacks from internet trolls.

↓

Greta protesting in Sweden in January 2020. Some people with similar conditions to Greta can feel isolated because of other people's prejudices.

↓

Rising above it

Unfortunately, Greta's experiences are very common for people who are different. People's prejudices and intolerance can make life challenging for them. Greta is a great role model for embracing our differences and seeing them as something positive. It takes a lot of strength to overlook personal attacks, especially at such a young age.

In denial

Some people, including high-profile leaders and journalists, are climate change deniers. They claim not to believe the science behind climate change and insist that humans aren't responsible for global warming. It's hard to know whether these people truly aren't convinced, or if they are using it as an excuse to continue getting rich from activities that pollute the environment, such as selling fossil fuels.

One of Greta's key phrases is 'Unite behind the science'. Supporting and raising awareness of the proven scientific evidence that suggests humans are responsible for climate change is very important so that climate change deniers can't mislead people.

↓

THE FIVE LARGEST FOSSIL FUEL COMPANIES SPEND NEARLY US$200 MILLION EVERY YEAR LOBBYING POLITICIANS TO DELAY, CHANGE OR STOP POLICIES THAT HELP FIGHT AGAINST CLIMATE CHANGE.

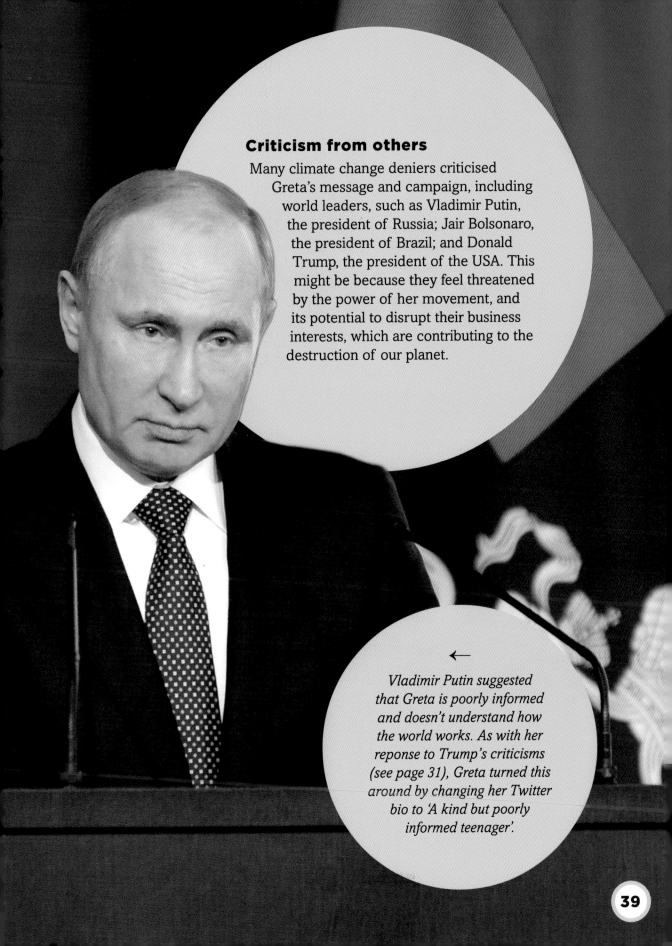

Criticism from others

Many climate change deniers criticised Greta's message and campaign, including world leaders, such as Vladimir Putin, the president of Russia; Jair Bolsonaro, the president of Brazil; and Donald Trump, the president of the USA. This might be because they feel threatened by the power of her movement, and its potential to disrupt their business interests, which are contributing to the destruction of our planet.

←

Vladimir Putin suggested that Greta is poorly informed and doesn't understand how the world works. As with her reponse to Trump's criticisms (see page 31), Greta turned this around by changing her Twitter bio to 'A kind but poorly informed teenager'.

IT'S NOT TOO LATE

Greta and other climate activists are very clear in their message – we can stop further damage to our planet, but we have to act now. We can't waste any time, as the longer we leave it, the more permanent, irreversible harm we will do and the more future generations will suffer.

End emissions now

The most important step in dealing with the climate crisis is to reduce greenhouse gas emissions dramatically and immediately. We must quickly replace fossil fuel power plants with greener alternatives, such as solar, wind and hydropower plants. Governments also need to invest in eco-friendly transport options, such as electric vehicles, and heavily tax people who continue to use vehicles that emit large amounts of emissions.

'THE MAIN SOLUTION ... IS SO SIMPLE THAT EVEN A SMALL CHILD CAN UNDERSTAND IT. WE HAVE TO STOP THE EMISSIONS OF GREENHOUSE GASES.'

GRETA THUNBERG, 2019

→ *Currently, wind, solar and hydropower generate about a quarter of the world's electricity. This amount will have to rise dramatically in order to reduce our use of fossil fuels.*

Not helping

Some places are waking up to the urgency of the situation and declaring climate emergencies, such as the EU, UK, Portugal, France, Canada and Argentina. But the climate crisis is the whole world's responsibility. Some countries are not doing their part and are actively ignoring the crisis. In the USA, climate scientists are being censored and in Turkey, there are plans to build 80 new coal power plants.

COUNTRIES THAT ARE TRYING TO TACKLE THE CRISIS

Sweden has committed to becoming 100 per cent fossil fuel free by 2050.

Since 2014, 95–98 per cent of Costa Rica's electricity has come from renewable sources.

The world's largest concentrated solar farm has been built in Morocco. It generates enough electricity to power two cities the size of its capital, Marrakesh.

9 out of 10 houses in Iceland are heated with renewable geothermal energy. Nearly 100 per cent of the electricity used in the country comes from renewable sources.

Climate justice

Some countries need to do more to help the environment than others. More economically developed countries are responsible for most of the activity that has caused the climate crisis, so it seems fair that they should be held mostly responsible for fixing the problem.

Unfair consequences

To make matters worse, it is less economically developed countries that are suffering most as a result of global warming, as their economies often depend on agriculture, which is heavily affected by extreme weather. Less economically developed countries can't afford the new technology needed to cut emissions, such as new power plants. More economically developed countries must financially support less economically developed countries to help them become more eco-friendly and recover from the effects of the climate crisis.

'THE BIGGER YOUR CARBON FOOTPRINT IS, THE BIGGER YOUR MORAL DUTY. THE BIGGER YOUR PLATFORM, THE BIGGER YOUR RESPONSIBILITY.'
GRETA THUNBERG, 2019

→ *The Turkana community in Kenya are struggling to grow crops because of continuous droughts due to climate change.*

Protecting the poles

Some scientists are developing new ways to protect our precious ecosystems from climate change while we try to get global warming under control. One plan is to try to protect polar habitats by spraying the ice with microscopic reflective 'sand'. The sand reflects heat outwards rather than absorbing it into the ice.

Another option could be to pump extra water on to the ice at the poles in the winter. This water will freeze, building up the thickness of the ice to counteract melting in the warmer summers.

Scientists monitor the sea ice at different times of year to see how it is being affected by climate change.
↓

THE ARCTIC COULD BE FREE OF ICE DURING THE SUMMER BY 2030 IF GLOBAL WARMING CONTINUES.

Replanting forests

Reforestation is another way to reduce the amount of greenhouse gases in the atmosphere. Trees absorb carbon dioxide from the atmosphere and store it. If we planted trees on a massive scale, it would help to reduce the greenhouse effect. Replacing wild trees also helps to encourage biodiversity (see page 19), which is being lost as a consequence of climate change and habitat destruction.

There are already tree planting programmes, such as the Bonn Challenge, which aims to restore 350 hectares of forest worldwide by 2030, but progress is slow.

↓

'RIGHT NOW, WE ARE IGNORING NATURAL CLIMATE SOLUTIONS. WE SPEND 1,000 TIMES MORE ON GLOBAL FOSSIL FUEL SUBSIDIES THAN ON NATURE-BASED SOLUTIONS.'

GRETA THUNBERG, 2019

PLANTING A TRILLION TREES WORLDWIDE COULD REMOVE UP TO TWO-THIRDS OF THE CARBON EMISSIONS IN THE ATMOSPHERE.

Greta's impact

Some people claim that making changes to your lifestyle is the best way of fighting back against the climate crisis. Small, individual actions, such as turning off unnecessary lights or walking to work, can help but they are not the solution to this problem. Greta's activism has helped to prove that coming together for large-scale actions and protests has a much greater impact than working alone.

Greta's story shows that we all have the power to make a difference by speaking up for what we believe in and coming together with others to make a stand.

→

Thinking bigger

Politicians and big businesses are responsible for this problem and they must lead the way by making significant, immediate changes to our economies and energy sources. We can help pressure them by taking part in protests, such as Greta's global climate strikes. Adults should vote carefully and choose candidates who will take climate change seriously.

'THE BIGGEST DANGER IS NOT INACTION. THE REAL DANGER IS WHEN POLITICIANS AND CEOS ARE MAKING IT LOOK LIKE REAL ACTION IS HAPPENING, WHEN IN FACT ALMOST NOTHING IS BEING DONE, APART FROM CLEVER ACCOUNTING AND CREATIVE PR.'

GRETA THUNBERG, 2019

Changing history

Greta's story is proof that we all have the power to create real change on a global scale. In a matter of months, Greta's passion for raising awareness of the climate crisis catapulted her protest from the streets of Stockholm to the front pages of newspapers around the world, inspiring millions of people along the way. Her hard work has started a global discussion on the climate crisis going forwards and has hopefully changed the course of history for the better.

GLOSSARY

atmosphere – the layer of gases around Earth

biodiversity – the variety of different plants and animals on Earth

deforestation – cutting down trees and clearing the land

drought – a period when there isn't enough water

ecosystem – all the living things in an area

emission – an amount of gas that is released

fossil fuel – a fuel that comes from the ground, such as coal, oil or gas

geothermal – connected to the heat inside Earth

greenhouse effect – the effect when certain gases gather in Earth's atmosphere, trapping the Sun's heat close to the surface and making it warmer

greenhouse gas – a gas that traps heat in the atmosphere, such as carbon dioxide

hydropower – using moving water to generate electricity

lobby – to try to persuade a politician or the government to do, or not do, something

ratify – to make an agreement official

reforestation – replanting trees to create a new forest

renewable – describes something that can be reproduced or will not run out

selective mutism – a condition where a person is unable to speak in certain situations, but they can speak in others

treaty – a formal agreement between countries

FURTHER INFORMATION

Further Reading

Eco Stories for Those who Dare to Care by Ben Hubbard (Franklin Watts, 2020)

Climate Change (Ecographics) by Izzi Howell (Franklin Watts, 2019)

This Book Will (Help) Cool the Climate by Isabel Thomas (Wren and Rook, 2020)

Websites

www.fridaysforfuture.org

Follow the FridaysforFuture protests and see if there are any events in your local area.

**www.natgeokids.com/nz/kids-club/cool-kids/general-kids-club/
greta-thunberg-facts**

Discover ten fun facts about Greta Thunberg!

**www.ted.com/talks/greta_thunberg_the_disarming_case_
to_act_right_now_on_climate_change?language=en**

Watch Greta Thunberg's TED talk about her climate strikes.

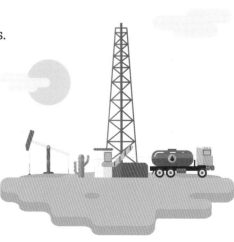

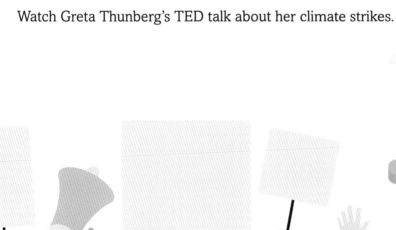

INDEX